MESSAGES

Rita Thompson

ISBN 979-8-89309-195-3 (Paperback)
ISBN 979-8-89309-196-0 (Digital)

Covenant Books
11661 Hwy 707
Murrells Inlet, SC 29576
www.covenantbooks.com

CONTENTS

Prologue vii

Part 1

    I Am...3

    Beloved 4

    Within 5

    Ordinary 7

    Spirit 8

    Gift 9

    Eternal 10

    Unspoken...11

    Searching..13

    Answers...14

    Whisperings 15

    Moments in Time 16

    Thee..17

    Grace...18

    Path...19

    Strength 20

    Angels 21

    Prayer of Protection....................................22

    Broken 23

    Peace 25

    Journey's End 27

    Embrace..28

    I Walk 30

    Breath 31

    Acceptance (a Message) 33

    Purpose 34

    The Seed 36

    Lost...37

Pure of Heart 39

Embers 40

Pages 42

A Gathering of Doves 44

Glory 46

The Infinite 48

Gardens 49

Divine Radiance 51

Messages...52

Spirit Dance 53

Kindred...54

Acorn 55

Dragonflies...56

You Are Heard..57

Messages...58

His 59

In His Light 61

Loving Grace..62

Lifted 63

View of Faith..64

Portions..65

Part 2

Growing..69

My Father's Words..70

Whisper My Name..72

Illusions..73

Butterflies...75

Wildflower 77

Once I Heard a Flower Dying 78

Portrait...80

Windows...81

Reaching Hands 82

Childhood Dreams...83

Delusions 85

Shadows of Reflection 86

Eveslace...88
A Time of Coming 91
Red Sun 93
Daybreak..94
Age...96
Trains and Cowboys 98
Ghost Town 100
The Old Man's Tale...101
Shadows on the Wall 103
Leaves..104
Blue Lace...105
All the Children 106
The Gift...107
Only Reflections 108
Forever and Always...109
Mazes 110
The Mist 111
Childless Moon 113
Eulogy..114
The Night of the Sun 115
The Trees of Time 116
Love Shadows..117
The Gladiators 118
Wisteria...119
Autumn...121
Julie...122
The Silence 123
Christy 125
A Friend, Mother 126
Circles of Love 127
The Rapture...129
Troubled Words 130
More than You Could Ever Know 132
Beyond the Barrier 134
Death Song..135
Star Child...137

His Gift..138
The Painting 139
Selfish Moon..140
Mirror, Mirror..142
A Birthday Wish 144
Stardust..145
Echoes of Silence...146
Poet..147
I See, but Do Others? 148
Andromeda 150
Rainbows 151
The Storm...152
Wild Child..154
True Love 155
One Moment 156
A Bird, a Tree, the Sky, and a Song 159
Child of the Wind..160
Words 161

PROLOGUE

Hear

These, the messages of angels,
Speaking the voice of God
Through His loving grace,
Gifted upon the feathered wings,
Lifting our souls heavenward
To the eternal Light.

None shall hear, lest they open their heart.
For His voice is calling us,
Calling to reach into our very souls,
Opening each to the sounds of His Love for us,
Guiding each of us along the path given us.
Hear the sounds He speaks
In every bird that sings to us.
Every chime rings out His Love.
Feel the calling of His Love,
Caressing us with each soft breeze,
Surrounding us with His loving embrace,
Whispering His grace softly in your ear.
Hear, and see His glory,
Blessing us each moment of this precious gift He has given us.
Each breath He has breathed into our very soul,
He has gifted us with a precious gift of life.
We are eternally His.
We are children of God,
Child, child of God,
Blessed are thee.

PART 1

I AM

The deafening silence grows loud, louder,
Encompassing my very being.

Its ravenous flow gnaws,
Ever growing stronger and stronger.

Each moment that passes,
Fleeting as it may be,
Time lingers endless in its ripples.
Waves rush over me, flowing,
washing away my soul.

An ember ever so slight,
Flickers of hope in desperation's grasp,
Promises of a greater Light,
The warmth of His loving embrace.

BELOVED

Cherished are the treasures we possess in our hearts,
Deeply nestled within each laugh, each tear.
Love and joy shall never part,
Kept deeply within the memories of
our souls held so dear.

As time shall quickly flow by,
Those loved and revered,
We hold each more precious; so hard we try
To release those thoughts so feared.

Each of life's single moments
Gathered as the flowers of the field,
Touched by the Light's true lament.
Love's strength shall never yield.

Beloved are all who we touch,
The eternal connection never ending in its Light,
Those in our hearts, we will ever clutch
Till the angel's winged flight.

WITHIN

The gift of time's grace,
Through love's sweet embrace,
Shall carry us upon its wings,
Through what each day may bring.

In our hearts, we shall hope.
Through each moment, our souls can cope.
The words of each friend, we hold dear,
If only to just hear.

God's love shall embrace us each one.
Believe in the gift of His Son.
For there shall be no fear,
Nor shall there be tear.

Laughter's sweet song,
In our lives it does belong.
Strong is our will to be,
Through the Light within you shall see.

Through hope, love, strength of will,
The Light of time shall stand still.
Each moment, each grace of time,
In our hearts we hold sublime.

The gift of time, each moment we live,
all is His gift to give,
Ours to hold in good measure,
Our most precious treasure.

We seek but only to find
In our thoughts that ever so bind.
No further need we seek,
Than within our hearts so meek.

The Light shall shine
Within each so divine,
Only to remind,
We need only look within to find.

ORDINARY

Uniqueness cannot fathom the caverns of simple thought,
Reaching deeply within the darkness for naught.

Time after time,
Each attempt, each rhyme,

Falls silent upon the thoughts; though we may try
Through the oneness upon which we rely,

We cannot meet the expectation,
Though each and every relation,

Though each sensation of our quest of summation
Could not and would not form such an expectation.

Our goals we strive to achieve,
Most grand, our dreams we believe

Can only cloud our vision we seek,
The veil dimming and bleak.

Although we are destined, we think,
Our greatness can be achieved in only a blink,

Yet in the universe of thought, we may place our query,
We are one, we are small, we are only ordinary.

SPIRIT

Spirit of Love, Spirit within,
if we could only begin
To see that which is around,
A glow with its ever-loving Light to astound,
Embraced in the Light of His Love,
Gracing us each from above.
The joy in our hearts' will thus grow,
Spreading the seeds of Love we sow.
Each that we touch
Will spread as such,
Gifting the power, He shall give
Within each soul to live.
The word that is spoken
Shall never be broken,
Always etched within our heart.
Through His grace, it will never part.
Always within,
Beyond the forgiven sin,
The Light shines bolder than the brightest star.
His blessings never far,
Each moment we shall seek.
With a heart so meek,
His Love we cherish true,
A blessed gift to me and you.
Forever, deep within,
We need only begin.
Seek within, we will do,
Only to find what is the most true,
His Love will always be,
For all we have to do is see.

GIFT

No matter what each day shall bring,
The gift of life will sing.
The birds that twitter,
Never could they be bitter.
Their song alive and bright,
For each to hear, a delight,
Warm and grand, a sight we see.
Each flower beckons you to be.
Embraced within its love,
A true gift from above,
The grace and beauty,
The fragrance surrounds and sets you free.
Behold that which is around you.
There you will find its love so true.
Deep within your heart,
Always to be a part,
The gift He has given, so right,
Forever our hearts delight.
His warm embrace you will feel,
His love that is always so real.

ETERNAL

Each time we see beyond,
Each time we know that which is
Within the heart of hearts, we grow fond,
Encompassed by the Light that is His.

Time can only be seen,
A far greater gift than we could comprehend.
Beyond each moment we glean,
His Love He will send.

Enfolding us with His loving embrace,
Forever safe and loved,
Surrounded with His Light and grace,
His children that are beloved.

Those that give of the heart,
Are eternally graced.
His Love shall never part
Through each trouble faced.

Forever He stands beside and within each one,
We that are a part
Of the heavenly Son,
All are of one eternal heart,

By the brilliance of His Light,
Forever we are embraced
And protected by His might.
Never our souls can be erased.

UNSPOKEN

Time endless in its quest,
Simplicity at its best,
Cannot fathom what we seek to know,
Yet in infinite wisdom of fate, it will show.

Each moment, each second, we live,
Time, the gift we give,
Can only be seen, only be felt,
By our knowing as we have knelt.

The Light for which we reach,
The blessings it shall teach,
Always present, always near,
That in our hearts we will never fear.

In our hearts we keep,
Each thought, each feeling so deep,
Will not be forsaken,
Nor can it be taken.

One, yet a part of the multitude,
Caught forever in each mood,
Left within our souls unspoken,
Forever a token.

The gift so gracious as it's given
Leads us to the path of heaven,
The Eternal Light,
Forever it shines ever so bright.

Enfolding us in its loving arms,
Ever caring, ever warm,
Always gentle in its embrace,
Its strength and love we can never replace.

Omnipotent in His Love,
Surrounding all from above,
With the golden Light to heal,
No other joy could we feel.

His Love ever so deep,
Washing us with tears, He shall forever weep,
To grow, to hope, to see,
Forever to be…

SEARCHING

Hope, the ever-present hand of God,
Guiding us in infinite wisdom,
Though we forever prod,
Can never be known to some.

Each one, each moment,
We can only seek,
Our hearts never content
In our quest ever bleak.

We dream,
Our hearts ever searching.
The unreachable, it would seem,
Our souls forever seeking.

Time fleeting as it may be,
Faster and faster, it does fly.
Beyond our reach, we do not see.
Upon our hearts, we must rely.

Always and forever by our side,
In His grasp, loving and strong,
By His truth, we do abide,
In His kingdom, we do belong.

The Light of His glory
Surrounds us as we seek to reach
Our never-ending story,
Forever the lesson He will teach.

ANSWERS

Blessed are those that know what was, that which is, and will be,
One moment, a blink of time,
For only those who shall see,
The lost and broken rhyme.

We seek through eyes of sight
But need only with our heart to know
The answer shining bright
Through that which we sow

Can only, through the soul,
Become that which we seek.
The towering bells, they will toll
For the weary and the meek.

In time we shall find no answer,
Yet in time there are all,
Eternity, a gift, a multitude of treasures.
Before our eyes, we place the wall.

To open the mind,
We need only try,
Feel that which will remind
And be on what we rely.

The answers we do seek
Can only be known to each.
In our hearts so meek
Are always here as He does teach.

WHISPERINGS

More and more precious each moment becomes, it would seem,
Softly whispering in the far reaches of the mind,
No more than a passing dream,
Still unknown, yet to each we do bind.

Farther and farther, we travel.
Our quest through unknown
Pulls us on the mystery to unravel.
Never are we alone.

Always at our side,
He guides us hand in hand,
His Love we ever abide.
Lovingly embraced with each stride so grand.

Ever-present in His grace,
His Love never ending by His giving,
Shine upon His brilliant face,
Reflecting within the precious gift of living.

His soul ever present within each,
Blessed are those who seek.
Our heavenly home we shall reach,
Though life may seem bleak.

MOMENTS IN TIME

Our love is endless in its reach.
There are no boundaries for any to say.
Many are the sands of the beach.
The ripples send waves to wash our woes away.

Each moment brings what it may.
Always a trial it will be.
Time stands firm, whatever at bay,
Though each veil we must see.

Moment to time, time to moment,
Blessings they all are.
Believe as they are sent,
Each a shining star.

Guiding us on our path,
Though we may not see,
Each a lesson born not of wrath,
But a gift to set our souls free.

Chains that bind us in our ways
Can only be broken.
Each link, through our fear, it stays,
Are torn only by the words He has spoken.

THEE

Thee,
A gift no other can see,
Blessed are those that have sight,
In their eyes You shine bright.
Guiding through the darkness,
Those with Your Light You bless,
Ever to be unfolded by Your Love,
A true gift from above.

Each word,
Each message spoken,
The trill of a bird,
A promise unbroken,
Cannot be heard,
Cannot be taken,
That which is the heart's true word
Will not be forsaken
Beyond that which cannot be broken.
Those who have seen will have discovered
The precious gift awoken.
In their hearts, the Light shall be heard,
Yet far beyond what we can comprehend
Lies an ever-present ray.
Time has no end,
Guiding us through each day.

GRACE

Time has no boundary for the wary
Thy Love transcends all,
Our souls thou dost carry,
Through the grace of Thy love, we can never fall.

Each moment, as it does seem,
Will carry us on our path.
Our lives to redeem,
For in thy Love, there is no wrath,

The sun shines bright,
Skies the brightest of blue,
Carry the Love of the Light,
Reflecting its heavenly hue.

Each laugh, each tear we cry,
All a precious gift
From heaven on high,
Our souls it does lift.

Aware we need be,
His Love so sublime.
With our hearts we must see
The Light from His Love divine.

His Light reflects in our faces
To give to all that can see,
With His loving grace,
Our souls shall be free.

PATH

Through each moment we seek thy face,
In our minds, the image we trace.
Forever through our gaze,
The answers always amaze,
Only from our hearts, we forever seek,
Though times may seem bleak.
No matter the trials we do endure,
You are always there to be sure.
We need only look within
The loving gift to begin,
To believe deeply from within our souls
Through each trial that takes its toll.
The everlasting love, forever to embrace
The shining Light from Your face.
It guides us on our path, winding it does seem,
Our faith, our souls to redeem
Trust from our very being,
The truest gift of seeing.
Thy voice rings true in our ear,
Stronger than any fear.
Through all darkness shines Your Light
Eternally bright!

STRENGTH

That which we know,
Forever and always shall be,
Through all we grow,
Through all we begin to see.

Time, ever-present in our mind,
Shadows over our soul,
Cloud the vision we seek to find,
Obscuring the path to our goal.

The Light we receive,
Given unto us each day,
In our hearts we believe,
With our strength, the darkness it shall allay.

The Light shines within.
No longer do we try.
No longer is there sin,
For in our hearts, we sigh.

The veil of darkness is lifted.
Stronger shines the Light.
His Love freely gifted
Through heaven's delight,

No more is there any worry.
Through His Love, our Light grows.
Through His Love we now see
The seeds of life He sows.

ANGELS

Angels of the Light,
Radiant and bright,
Keep us through the night,
Protect and keep us from harm
That there shall never be cause for alarm.
Surround us with your guidance and protection
Through darkness and sun.
So be it, and so it is done.

Prayer of Protection

Of many colors is a rose
Of protection, I propose.
Surround this property as a haven,
Magic guard us by the call of the raven.
Let there be no cause of alarm.
Guard and protect us from all harm.
Surround us with healing and prosperity.
I beseech Thee with great sincerity.
By the moon's light and the owl's cry,
Goodness and Light be ever nigh.

BROKEN

Our days are long,
Wrought with sadness,
No longer we feel we belong,
Feeling no longer needed and useless.

We gaze but cannot see.
Dimness clouds our eyes.
What is it we need to be,
Weighed down by the lies.

No longer are we aware.
No longer do we feel.
Greeted by the stare,
Through numbness we appeal.

Much we have lost.
Our souls no longer see the Light.
At what is the cost,
We have lost our sight.

We call to the One,
Our voices cry out.
Lost and weak, we beseech the Son.
We call through our doubt.

Help us to see,
Help us to know.
Our hearts yearn to be,
Yet He cannot bestow.

What we must receive,
The choice we must do.
The gift is freely given but only to believe,
If only to be taken, we can make it so.

Totally we are forgiven; forever it is His.
Never to be forsaken,
A Love beyond all that is,
It can never be taken.

We must receive,
What is eternally His.
We must first believe,
For simply it is.

PEACE

Each moment, I think of You.
My heart yearns to see the Light.
Clouds clutter my mind, not letting You through,
Dimming my sight.

I forget the truth beneath each worry.
You are always there.
My mind in such a hurry,
Cannot see how much You care.

Each drop of rain that falls
Carries my woes away,
For I see from my heart that calls,
The words I cannot say.

Within each moment that I live,
My thoughts deceive me.
So much Love You have to give,
I cannot always see.

Stop in a moment of peace,
Bask in the Light freely given.
All of time will cease,
No longer are we driven.

Our hearts glow with His Love,
Renewed by the Light of His glory.
Blessed from above,
We continue our story.

Though long and arduous is our task,
He guides us on our journey.
Deeply in His Love we bask,
Forever in our hearts we shall then see.

No greater a gift is given,
The Light of His Love,
Truly from heaven,
His glory from above.

Journey's End

The gift that He has given,
Time graces us each.
All that we are and have been are forgiven,
His Love we do beseech.

No limits are there placed,
All-encompassing is His Love.
Through all the trials faced,
Born upon the wings of a dove.

Graceful in its flight,
It carries us through.
We seek our path true and right,
With a belief we must renew.

The answers we seek, forever binding,
Our path we travel never ending,
His Love always reminding,
Of the truth and Love He is sending.

Our hearts see what it is,
The journey is at its end.
We are no more, no less than His,
No more shall we pretend.

The truth we seek is at hand,
Our souls shine with His Light.
The darkness forever banned,
The eternal Love eternally bright.

EMBRACE

Each time we feel lost,
Our hearts are darkened without the Light.
How sorrowful, at what cost,
His Love never fades from sight.

Eternally He has given,
A Love forever there,
Though our hearts are driven
With a mindless stare.

Within, deeply there is an ember,
Ever so slight it is,
If only to remember
The Love that is His.

Each moment we falter and fall,
He is there to catch us.
In our souls we must recall,
No queries need we discuss.

Time unending in its plea,
Carries us through,
Its strength and wisdom ever to be,
A Love, forever and true,

It encompasses us all
A warm and loving embrace,
With its never-ending call,
A blessing filled with grace.

Eternally it speaks,
Always in our hearts,
Seen through the souls of the meek,
A strength never to part.

We are a part of thee,
Thou art a part of us each.
If in our hearts and souls we see,
Deep within we must reach.

We seek ever to find
The touch that is always there.
With a Love so beautiful and kind,
Our souls, we must be aware.

We seek His truth and Love,
Stop and listen to the word,
The message always from above,
The answers, you have already heard.

Within each heart,
On our path we are led.
His Love, never shall it part,
With His words He has said.

I WALK

I walk within the Light of His glory
With each step I take.
He guides me.
Hand in hand we travel.
Our journey, guided by His Love,
Each moment, each mile we travel.
No task is so daunting,
No trial too hard to bear.
His Light guides me through the darkness.
Ever-present is He beside me.
He holds me so I do not fall.
We seek the road less traveled,
The road on which others have since found their way.
No matter our fears, nor our unbelief,
He carries us, lifting our souls to a higher knowing.
We then see, through the eyes He has gifted us, through His eyes,
To see, truly see, who we are.
We are born His creation
Through His loving grace,
Forever in His heart,
Forever in His Light.

BREATH

With each breath we exhale,
Time stands still.
In our endeavors, we must not fail.
We must have strength of will.

Waver, we must not,
To find is our goal.
Through wisdom we have been taught
What is our true role,

The words speak their message,
As they are said and heard.
We travel each our own passage
Upon each and every word.

Life, an adventure traveled,
A journey profound,
Our lives though unraveled,
Guide us each to where we are bound.

Our path predestined as they wrote
In the Book of Time,
With each and every quote
Guided by the gift of rhyme.

We seek and will find
Our soul's place in time,
Enfolded in His embrace, ever so kind,
A true gift of the sublime.

Each breath we take,
Its rhythm speaks its rhyme.
With each step we take,
We keep our place in time.

The blessings of life's sweet melody,
We embrace each moment.
With this gift we truly see
All that is, is heaven-sent.

ACCEPTANCE (A MESSAGE)

It is not ours to comprehend. It is ours but to take the journey. As we think, say, and do, it is a constant…a lesson each moment we live. Many cannot and will not learn. Their minds are closed to the infinite possibilities that are. Many think only they know what is right and that it is only their way. It is not ours to judge another's worth but to accept each for who they are. And pray that they accept their path to be deemed by God. It is His will and Love that carry us. We must accept this gift, for it is of the highest intent, filled with great blessings and Light. The more we believe and know by our hearts and souls, the more we are as we were created to be. Our very beings are thus filled with a greater Love and Light, spilling over with joy to give to others and to be thankful thereof.

PURPOSE

Deep within the reaches of the mind
Lies an ever-eternal voice.
Listen deeply, and there you will find
The gift of choice,

Within each thought,
The answer lingers endlessly.
Hanging upon the tasks we have wrought
Until in our hearts we shall see.

Each moment we shall live,
In our hearts lies the questions we have sought.
Our gift we shall give
Freely from our souls without thought.

His Light encompasses all,
Forever a forgiving love.
Though many times we shall fall,
Always He guides us from above.

No longer is time the question.
The answers, they are known.
Our path is finally done.
We now reap the love we have sown.

Guiding us all along our way,
The time has now come.
It is a bright and new day,
Heralding the Light we have become.

Our journey is never at end,
For on a new path, we continue.
On a new life He does send,
Always a lesson that is due.

The Light shall always shine,
Forever to enfold us.
His loving embrace sublime,
Now we are with His purpose.

THE SEED

Memories blessed with the kiss of the past,
Endearing, reaching into the depths of time.
Held gentle within each tear to last
Are cradled within the ever-eternal rhyme.

Searching each day, each hour,
Seemingly lost within the wave,
We seek the ultimate power,
Weakness, against which to stave.

With faint heart,
Unending, it does seek.
The soul to never part,
Ever and always, it seems bleak.

Within the Light grows,
Sparking to its eternal flame,
Its ember ever grows,
The soul to never be the same.

Each day we see more clearly.
In our eyes we now know.
His Love grows more dearly.
The seed He has planted does now grow.

LOST

The emptiness engulfs me,
Deafening in its echoes.
I call your name but do not see,
Deeply falling into my woes.

They surround my being,
Enveloping me tighter and tighter.
There is no freeing.
The Light is no longer brighter.

The silence rings out loud.
My soul aches
Covered by the ever-darkening cloud,
Waiting, waiting till my soul awakes.

I called and called, but now it's too late.
My heart gave up too soon.
I know not your fate,
But I ever wait by the light of the moon.

I implore you, Spirit.
I seek your divine grace.
As I gaze at the candle I have lit,
Its light embraces your face.

I seek but do not find.
Your light grows ever dimmer.
My love for you does ever bind,
Seeking to glance even a glimmer.

I pray your light be ever bright.
Forever you are in my heart.
Though your love fades from sight,
Our souls will never be apart.

PURE OF HEART

I give truly of my heart.
I give the love I have received.
Love that is true shall never part,
A gift from a love that is believed.

A heart open to give
Can only become that which is
The knowledge from which we live
That can only be His.

Each moment that is
Each moment we perceive
Can only be His.
Always at our side, His love we need only receive.

A giving heart, truly blessed,
Can only give as is given.
A reflection at its best,
As the golden threads were woven.

The simplest thought,
The purest of intent,
Freely given could never be bought,
Can only be heaven-sent.

EMBERS

'Twas a night long ago,
Silent and dark.
The cold winds they do blow,
In the fires, there's not even a spark.

Sleep has dulled my thought.
I dream dreams I cannot remember.
I know not what time has brought.
All is lost in the dying ember.

Sweet songs and laughter elude me.
The silence is overwhelming.
I can no longer see.
There is no song to sing.

Draped in the chilling cold,
I hunger for sustenance.
My eyes grow old,
Held by a timeless trance.

My mind, clouded, I remember not.
I see only, glimpses through the veil.
Not knowing what time has wrought,
Though I try, I fail.

I can no longer grasp what I seek.
I have become weak with anguish.
All seems so bleak.
Only to see the Light, I wish.

I long for a time when laughter was full,
Joy and love with its warming embrace.
My heart deeply feels the pull,
Longing for His heavenly grace.

A spark comes to life.
Ever brighter it grows.
No longer do I feel the strife,
Er the cold winds shall blow.

A fire within me fills my soul,
A warmth far beyond the flame.
With Its loving embrace I am whole,
Never to be the same.

PAGES

The message has come.
It speaks to me clear and true.
I hear the words; loudly they drum.
The stronger they grew.

The time has come it would seem,
An end, though, not so,
A new path as He would deem,
A new time to grow.

An end to the past,
A beginning to see,
A lifetime to last,
Now to be free.

The chains that binds are broken.
To now live and to feel
His Love has now awoken,
A gift given to heal.

Too long has it been,
The years, many and unending,
A lifetime lost, never again,
Life grows from the wound mending.

The wind calls to me,
Hugging, me with Your loving embrace.
The chains are now broken, and I see,
What has been lost is found in Your loving grace.

It has been and always will be,
Forever Your Love is given,
To open our eyes, our souls to see,
Always and forever are we forgiven.

A GATHERING OF DOVES

Their sweet, soft melody,
Memories of a time past,
A song of love, a gift to be,
A love forever to last.

Each rhyme they speak
Enfolds you with great love.
Though the world may seem bleak,
They carry a message from above.

Stop and hear their word,
Their sweet song they give,
As softly as none has heard,
A gift of life to live.

So simple, yet so sweet,
The message profound,
Time and again they repeat
Such a soft and soothing sound.

If only for a time
The soft flutter enfolds your soul,
A winged grace sublime,
Only to fulfill their role.

As we live our lives so short,
Time gives us its length of measure.
Life needs no retort,
For each moment we must treasure.

Fragile is its rhyme,
Though short it may be.
Our true place in time
From within, we must truly see.

GLORY

To be a soul's worth,
We need only view.
A gift from birth,
We need only do.

In a book of old it is written,
Our lives as gifted,
Each moment forever Lenten,
Etched deeply within our souls lifted.

In the Light of thy glory,
There can be no darkness.
In life's never-ending story,
With His eternal love, He does bless.

Each day we seek our lot
With each moment that passes.
In our hearts, we seem forever fraught,
Yet He, in His infinite love, forgive us our trespasses.

His love forever encompasses us,
Hugging us with His loving embrace.
To each He unfolds our purpose,
Forever blessed with the Light of His grace.

With each moment we open our eyes
To see the Light of His blessings.
The picture unfolds as the soul tries,
Focus, the angel sings.

See that which is His,
A gift forever given,
A love stronger than all that is,
With the strength of spirit, we are driven.

Time has no limit or domain,
Eternal is its span.
For always we shall remain,
Forever in His eyes is His plan.

Our souls forever a part
Sparks of His true love,
Truly a gift of His heart,
Always a part of...

THE INFINITE

Time is the essence of all things,
Each breath, each moment or thought,
All are one—past, present, future.
All are one of the exact same time,
Coexisting, being of the same, of the One,
The infinite, beyond that which is beyond,
anything we could ever understand.
None could ever fathom the enormity of life,
of thought, of being,
For beyond our grasp, the Light shines,
brighter than the spark of life, brighter than
the sun yet never blinding but all
encompassing, all omnipotent.
Its gentle, warm embrace wraps around us
in its splendor.
Each molecule, within the essence of all
that exists, through the ripples of time,
transcends all.

GARDENS

Angels appear, a multitude of shapes and sizes,
Each carried upon the breath of heaven,
Sudden surprises,
The soft puff of wind now and then.

The memory of a time long ago,
The soft fragrance remembered,
Along the path as we go,
Guided by the uplifting serenade of a bird.

Each moment, at any given time they bless.
Feel the soft flutter of their wings,
Embracing in a loving caress
As all of heaven sings,

Coral bells ring in the soft breeze.
Swaying gently are the chimes,
Ringing their melodies through the trees,
Heralding the ever-present rhymes.

Birds singing their symphony,
Twittering happily, they say
The day is bright and sunny,
Shining through the trees as they sway.

A quilt of many colors,
Blanketing the gardens,
Peace to the soul it offers,
God's true message of love it sends.

The sun glistens brightly,
Glittering gems of dew,
Reflecting ever so slightly,
Giving the gift to renew.

Peace of mind,
Peace of soul,
Through the loving Light you will find.
Embrace your true role.

Divine Radiance

No level of passion could fain the definition of love.
Deep within the caverns of the soul thus it dwells.
This gift, the eternal emotion,
More precious than life itself,
Infinite in its wisdom and grace,
By no coin nor jewel could it be purchased.
By no soul could it be bartered.

There are messages of wisdom from the heart,
Its yearnings mirroring the soul's needs.
The spirit needs the corporal gift of emotion
to enrich and teach it knowledge and wisdom,
The corporal needs, the knowing of spirit to guide
it to a greater existence of true being
of enlightenment and Light,
Ethereal Light,
Glorious in its radiance,
Encircles with its warmth,
Healing the soul within its divine love.

Messages...

Life goes on in its infinite patterns and
reflections entwining and weaving its
web of connection.
All life, all souls are connected as one.
We are all one-minute part of the grander scheme.
Our souls are ever linked by the golden thread.

The road to nowhere is short,
But the road to destiny is a long
and treacherous path.

Soft heart,
Soul weeps,
The eternal vigilance,
Angel's light,
Radiance of grace.

Spirit Dance

I am an eagle.
I soar with the spirits of the wind.
They carry my voice,
Cry out, Brother,
The sky is mournful.
Seek the beginning of the song.
Soar high with the eagle's dance.
Sing out through his cry,
Echoing His father's voice.
Seek the beginning.
Embrace the source.
Dance, feel the spirit within.
It flows freely,
Lifted on the air.
The rhythm speaks.
Its words flow,
Ripples, endless in their journey,
Back to that which began,
That which created spirit.
It speaks words known only to the souls of time,
Transforming into the Light,
Seeking the One,
Knowing the I Am.

KINDRED

A timeless traveler,
Ancient, yet ageless,
Through many lifetimes our lives have touched.
Our paths entwined, forever to meet
Many faces, mirrored through the eyes of the soul.
Always a feeling of the familiar
Kindred souls we are,
Time has no boundary, no limit to our beginning, nor our ending,
For time is endless.
Forever we are bound.
We are ever joined in the dance of time,
A lifetime, many times, again and again.
Our souls are linked,
For we are one.
We are from the One,
A spark of His Love.
We are a part of the Source,
The Source a part of each,
We are but One.

ACORN

Through times ages I stand tall.
Strong and grand I spread my arms.
Reaching out, I implore,
Living grace of grandeur.
I sing to the winds,
Swaying to its lullaby.
My heritage I grant to thee,
An ever-changing, loving gift.
I give this to those who see,
Those who hear my song.
The heavenly melody I sing,
Lifting me to new heights,
Forever embracing me in its arms.
In silence I hear the melody,
Wafting through the air,
Softly, strongly, caressing my soul.
My heart dances to the rhythm,
Becoming one with its very soul,
Feeling, knowing, being as one,
I am thee!

DRAGONFLIES

I fall,
And you catch me.
I stumble,
And you steady me.
The birds sing their praises.
The butterflies flutter gracefully.
My heart is lifted upon the breeze.
Softly, I float,
Dancing to its melody.
Upon gossamer wings I soar.
Humming softly, I speak.
Silent words are spoken
But are heard.
I am seen.
I am loved.
My heart delights to the joyous laughter.
Happily, they dance,
Heralding the love embraced.
Life's light shines ever so bright,
Dancing upon the light's wonder.

You Are Heard

Speak to me, and I will listen.
Teach me, and I will know.
Each moment, I hear Your voice.
My heart soars in joyous anticipation.
Your love embraces me,
Calming my heart's anxieties.
Your love brings peace to my soul.
It enfolds me in its warm embrace.
I thus know You are always with me.
I trust Your loving word.
It fills my very being with the Light of Your countenance,
Always, You watch over us and protect us.
Never need we fear the unknown.
All is revealed with Thy grace,
Ever to be within us and around us.
Never are we alone,
For Your loving grace lifts us,
Surrounding us with Your loving Light.
Forever are we graced with Your loving presence.
Forever are we blessed.
Forever are we loved.
Forever are we heard!

MESSAGES

Sob,
Let the tears wash over you,
And love thy Father.
He makes the sky the bluest of blue.
There's no evil to bother.
The birds they do sing.
His voice is lifted upon the air.
Loudly His love rings.
Forever from His very being He does care.
His loving Light surrounds us,
Always at our side.
Believe it will be thus,
Our souls to abide.
His word strong and clear.
His voice, do not ignore.
In His heart, He holds us dear.
Only our love He does implore.

HIS

Blessings come in many ways,
Each a surprise,
Truly given, what may,
With each day the sun does rise.

Each moment we see more
Through His love that surrounds us.
He does truly adore.
His Light ever more glorious.

Surrounding us with its radiance,
Our very beings He does adore.
It be told not just once,
But through an eternity of blessings, we soar.

He has gifted us His life.
He has taken upon Himself our worries
And lifted our strife,
His ever-present love telling our stories.

Each moment we live,
His grace surrounds us.
With His loving Light He does give,
Blessing our each and every moment thus

We forever seek His love,
More and more we see,
He ever surrounds us from above,
Forever His we shall be.

Never is there a time to be distraught,
No matter the circumstances we face.
From each of us we must only seek
what is brought,
Truly given of His loving grace.

To our true home we shall go.
Our time, to each, our path is given.
It is written, we shall thus know
The truest gift, heaven.

IN HIS LIGHT

That which is and ever shall be,
The Light of Thy glory shines upon us,
Each and every moment your Light
bears witness to Thine glory.
Our hearts yearn for the strength
of your presence,
Deep within, our souls cling to You.
Ever present is Your loving grace,
Always at our side,
Always within us,
Beckoning, yearning to see You and to hear Your voice.
It rings out loudly, softly, ever in our beings,
Ever in our souls.
It warms the soul's emptiness,
Bringing back the life torn from us.
The eternal flame grows,
Sparking to life the embers waiting…
yearning to come to life again,
A new flame begins.
It grows, casting its radiance,
Encompassing all that we were,
are and shall be, ever in His Light.

LOVING GRACE

He does temper the winds of change.
Ever does He guide and protect us.
Our time, He has given in its due measure,
No one, nothing can ever take this from us.
No moment can be lost,
For it is given of Himself.
The eternal flame burns within each of us.
Eternally our souls are gifted.
We need only see His love He gives us.
Freely, openly, forever is His love.
None shall know His true glory.
None can comprehend its gravity, its grace.
Forever are we to learn, to seek.
Our gift He has given.
It is ever to be our path.
Our lives each a spark from His love.
Ever we seek the Light.
Ever we need His loving grace,
For we are ever a part of Him.
Ever we seek the stillness of His peace.

LIFTED

And so He speaks.
Our souls see the words spoken.
A bird's sweet song,
A flower in bloom,
The rays of sun shining upon us,
Each leaf, each blade of grass,
He speaks to us.
Hear His words
Feel them through your soul.
We ever seek to know His love.
We ever need His warming embrace.
No matter the day, nor the night,
He is ever present in each of us.
His Light grows stronger as we seek.
His Light shines ever brighter.
As we begin our journey of believing,
Listen, breathe in deeply His loving essence.
Feel His healing grace lift your weary spirit.
His strength enfolds you and protects you,
Surrounding you, transforming you.

VIEW OF FAITH

Christians, whether they be Jewish or of other
races and beliefs, have been persecuted since the
beginning of time, yet their strength, which
lies within their faith, cannot be diminished—
for they are as the sands in the wind,
a multitude, eternal in their vigil.

Time cannot conquer them, for their gift of
the Father is life eternal, more beautiful
than any can imagine. This is the most
cherished and revered gift of all time. No one
can just acquire this. It must be earned.
It is earned only through a life of diligence,
truth, honesty, faith in our Father—all
that is good and just in the eyes of the Lord.

Our lives are a constant test of our faith.
We only see it as bad luck that everyone
is out to destroy us, poverty and starvation
and a host of many other situations. Yet
only by our faith can we conquer our
own fears and trials and tribulations.
All it takes is faith—strong and sure
faith. Believe that is the key factor.

PORTIONS

See through the eyes of the blind man,
And you shall know.

The gifts of the pearl,
Iridescent in their mystery
Yet simple in their beauty,
Are deep in their contemplation.

Seek not the seeker
But those who contemplate.
For they have found.

Love is not a bed of roses.
Love is taking the thorns with the beauty.
Love is growing and sharing.
Love is sacrifice and understanding.
Love is truly caring.

God is!
Therefore I am,
For God created me.
His gift to me is life.
My gift to Him is my soul!

Patience be your raiment,
Understanding be your guide,
And faith be your reward.

Dreams—the eternal flame of the
rebirth of life.

Music—the song of God's love reaching forth
through an eternity of life reborn.

I seek Thee.
My soul searches
Through the passages of time,
Each corridor endless.
One unto another,
I am lost within.

Wouldst thou despair, so if it were not for your own being,
Come, partake of His soul, blessed with the eternal gift of love.

PART 2

GROWING

A child is born of innocence,
Pure and gentle.

Laughter fills the air of voice,
Drifting through the years of beginning.

Time brings forth many treasures of growing,
Awakening a new life of learning,
Of inquisitive questions,
Expressions of endearing love.

Too many times, the treasures slip away,
Coming of an age of awareness,
An age of heart,
But to never end in the fight to fulfill the hunger,
The search of self,
To see the time of coming,
The day of flight,
A new beginning of wonder,

More precious are the moments spent.
Each day, another dream come to life,
Mellowing memories of yesterday,
Though only tomorrow's past,
Through another lifetime,
A passing of time to endure,
Of innocence reborn,
The child born of innocence
Forever a treasure to be cherished,
For only once is this gift deemed.

My Father's Words

I bury my heart in sweat of brow to
toil and breathe life to the earth of time,
Shackled I can never be,
For I am born of the earth, and to the earth
I return sublime.

I spread seeds of love within the bosom of the earth.
They take root and grow,
Blooming forth the song of life,
bearing the fruits of labor's worth.

A labor of love it is, to see life unfold.
Oh, glorious a sight to see
But to know and feel that life within your soul,
No greater a gift could there be.

A painting of words were the first he wrote,
A picture rare of beauty
To ponder with thoughts remote.

The first I saw was short and simple,
for only simple he would live.
My thoughts go back to rediscover his love,
Reaching out to life, to me, to give.

He touched my heart with the words he spoke,
With his memories unspoken.
His love was so strong, never a heart he broke.

A tall man, young and alive,
I remember when,
Full of stories and poems,
A sweet voice that sang out each word in a melody never forgotten.

Now I see him no more but hear the laughter turn to tears.
No more can we walk hand in hand
And talk of our private fears.

A love so rare and true of heart, I can never lose to this day,
For in my heart, I hear him still.
My father's words, he'd say,

"Honey, when you walk this day and every day,
Listen to the laughter of the wind, and always
Keep the sunshine in your heart
To give to someone along the way."

He never took of other's lands
But only gave from his heart,
Working endlessly with his kind and patient hands.

WHISPER MY NAME

As I gazed upon the misty seas veiling the lands of dusk, I saw,
The moon, casting mysterious heaven, wrought lights,
Lighting the sky as a torch in the night,
Uplifted in mellow rivers of thought,
Rising forth from the earth to life.
It flowed softly around me, lifting me toward heaven.

Lay me to rest high above the mountain of the sun,
For this is my home, my heart, and soul,
Whisper my name upon the ends of the earth, and I shall live on immortal,
For I am born upon the wings of time,
Endless in a voyage through space.

I have planted my seed of love in the heart of mankind.
Now let it take root and flourish,
Unfold seed into life,
Rise with the breath of the morning mist,
Go forth in wisdom, and bring nations of glory to being.

Thrive not upon the matter of things,
But nourish upon the soul of spirit.
Grasp not a fleeting of a moment but a lifetime of eternal,
For he who seeks the truth, none shall be known,
Yet for he who walks in truth, all of wisdom shall be known.

ILLUSIONS

Nostalgic melodies embrace the air with scents of magnolia blossoms,
Childhood dreams of castles in the skies,
Rising above the amber light of dawn,
Of those passing stars caught on high.
Misty clouds of rainbows transcend high on wings of gossamer.
Rays of golden treasures shaft the misty veils,
Drifting aimlessly across the reaches of space,
Calling out sunny daydreams through my soul of time.

Castles of my mind,
What is real or unreal,
All are one illusion.
Life is but an illusion of existence,
An existence of illusion.

For I am but a traveler of time,
Existing only as a space in time,
Spreading my seeds on the winds of laughter,
Rustling through the leaves of life of the universe,
A twinkling of a star, the birth of a new life,
An existence brought forth from another time,
Another destiny,

Transcending all levels of time, all reaches of existence
Far beyond any limit of domain,
The soul of soul,
Heart of heart

Are only as visioned,
Clinging to myths and legends of past,
A presence of being without change,
A time to come yet has passed,
A millennium, spoken long ago.

For what is forever
But time revisited,
Time melted into one second,
Spread across an eternity of existence.

BUTTERFLIES

Pure as gentle flight of winged grace
Are refracted jewels of rainbow light,
Wavering above golden seas of ageless trace,
The messengers of eternal light

Of a time come to pass,
Grown of ageless wonder,
A moment, brief alas,
Yet never laid asunder.

For each are born of a child's dream,
Ever a cherished rhyme.
A treasure it would seem,
Buried upon innocence's mime,

Each a window of past,
Each a vision of to be,
No more, no less, to last
But only a glimpse to see,

Captured forever, yet of one moment,
Of each is a part.
The tears of angel's lament
Etched deeply in my heart.

Of the many treasures of time's land,
This the most beloved of children,
Gently held in hand,
Will never come again.

Yet with each memory comes a dream,
A time of past to relive,
The angel's gift to deem.
To another this moment to give.

WILDFLOWER

Gather ye, gentle maids,
Dancing to golden lyres round fairy mushrooms of misty blue.
Kiss their lips with honey.
Pierce their hearts with throngs of laughter.

Gather ye, merry men,
Round the cups of wine.
Sweeten their bodies with dew.
Bring smiles of love to their hearts.

Soft winds chime coral bells.
Sweet roses of dew entwine among the briar thorns.
Their strange melodies engulf your, mind, body, and soul,
Lifting them on the dimensions of time,
Drifting endlessly through the void of space.

Gentle serenades drift sweetly on the murmurs of time, unending,
Blossoming forth with the fruits of the earth.

Worlds bathed in mellow thoughts and sunshine,
Softly melt into silence…

ONCE I HEARD A FLOWER DYING

A time came when no longer was there any feeling, any rhyme, or reason.
I could no longer touch life.
Tomorrow is but yesterday—another day.
There were no hours or minutes,
No laughter or sorrow.

I could not see or speak.
There was nothing but nothingness itself.
Time has no eye for whom it strikes.
I know not for what my existence is,
For it merely is.

As I walked through the day of shadows,
I heard a flower dying.
It cries to me,
Its tears fell upon my heart, and I wept.

The trees bowed their heads in sorrow.
The fawn crept close.
The nightingale's plea went unanswered.

A great emptiness filled the air.
The flower wept softly, echoing in the silence.
I felt a hollow gnawing deep in my heart.

"Do not feel such sadness,
For I wept only for you.
For I cannot sing for you,
Cannot see you."

As the sun rose gently,
Light pierced the shadow and shone through the dark of the forest.
It fell upon the flower.

Laughter filled the air with the warmth of love,
Sparkling in the eyes of the flower.

My friend, speak not harshly of life.
For once, I heard a flower dying.

PORTRAIT

Eyes search deep into your very soul,
Golden as the amber light of dusk.
Your lips pursed in a gentle, thoughtful smile.,
Waves of golden light flow as a summer's day
Trailing to your shoulders pale.
Fragile works of art caress a rose fair.
Pressed close to your heart a flower, rivaled by your beauty's stare.

No strokes could tell of your secrets.
No other could tell of your desires.
It is but a breath of life to the mourning sigh,
Which haunts the echoing remnants,
Drowsy with the sleep of want
That bears the mysteries
Forever caught in time immortal.

WINDOWS

Wind crisp and strong,
Trees dancing to its song,
Leaves, no longer green,
Now somber, sighing, and unseen.

The sea no longer still,
The beach no longer gay,
The garden now bare and shrill,
Beauty no longer to array.

Winter is glinting
About every nook and crook
And burdening,
The shoulders of all the world to look.

No longer is there the warm lament,
The sun of yesterday,
My life a violent storm of torment,
Spiraling into the sky so gray.

Life seems so short.
I no longer know
Where lies my port,
Ere the wind shall blow.

REACHING HANDS

Torn between pride and hunger,
Old and weathered,
Leather in texture,
Kneeling before God,
Crying!
Begging!
A soul lost in a world of wealth,
Even below that that is lowest.

Though the sun shines bright with life,
This poor weary figure is frozen,
With her hands reaching to God!
No more the agony but a smile of peace on her face,
No more to beg for solace
But only daffodils fragrant with dew,
Wave their greeting of another life
In the heir of golden suns.

CHILDHOOD DREAMS

A coldness has come over me.
I can no longer feel the love
Nor see the reasons why.

Too many years of scratching for a living,
Too many years of running from myself,
Have left my life empty.
Cold dark silence is my companion,
Speaking to me in echoes of tears.

I see in the mirror no vision.
My eyes are deceived by a person
        I have never seen.
I only see the emptiness that grows,
For it is only the leaves that turn
        golden by my window.

Sitting in silence, I wander through
        my mind's eye,
Back to the years forever lost.
I hear the voices creep into the room,
Softly whispering my name.

My mind is filled with the laughter of
my children,
The pains of growing
All my plans and dreams.
My secret treasures of heart,
It all seems so very far away.

Lost in a haze,
Yet, somehow, I feel I'm there.
I see the old house,
Grandpa still sitting there on the porch.

I remember the day I left.
There were tears in his eyes.
He knew he'd never see me again.

How I wished then I could take away
        those tears,
I know in my heart I should stay,
But I was drawn to leave.

But now his eyes are filled with joy!
His smiles greet me warmly.
I no longer fear,
For I know I'm home again,
And I'll never leave.

DELUSIONS

Too many times, there are no limits to the
    agonies of the mind.
Each day, another peril arises,
Taxing the sanity of one's reality.
Or is it the reality of one's sanity?
Confrontation after another weakens the core.
Society, the epitome of the disease,
Grows, closing in,
Pressuring from all sides
Yet pulling in all directions.
Threatened, the mind retreats into its chambers,
Seeking safety from the enemy,
Forever scarred, an outcast,
A no-man, searching for a home but finding none,
A world of fantasy, a world of agonizing expectation,
    of what no one knows,
Eats away until fear is the only reality.
An unknown terror grasps the mind,
Trapping the body in another world,
A world known only to the mind's eye,
So removed yet more defined than ever before
    in light of reality,
More real than a life, which stifled the soul to
    almost total annihilation.
To escape was the only alternative,
To advance into a more evolved state of existence known by few
Yet for some, less than life,
A tomb woven of their own designs.
But those who cling to this reality called society
Are caught in a timeless whirlpool
With no escape from their delusions.

SHADOWS OF REFLECTION

Of my love I write,
For no other was so precious to me.

Each day, more dear than the last, I see him
        again in my heart,
And my love is renewed and deepened.
The memories flow into my mind,
Overwhelming me to tears.

The moments we spent together, though few they were,
Could never embitter my heart.
For though my love is gone,
He is forever with me.

The days pass into mirrors of reflection,
Haunting me with the things I can never forget.
Though time has lessened the pain,
Nothing could remove the scars left in my heart.

The roses have grown full of life,
Their thorns their guardians,
To protect the fragile breath of angel's wings,
Touched with the tears of heaven,
Each a reflection of time,
For a moment stands still,
The eternal gift of lovers.

Ageless are the seas,
Though strong is the longing to be free,
Freedom from the bondage of heart,
The loneliness growing inside of me.

I struggle within,
My heart not to be comforted.
Each day I arise, more aware of the discontent
        growing stronger.
It greatly saddens me,
For I am torn in many directions,
Searching for some kind of peace.

Though I feel no bitterness for the loss,
I can never lose the shadows of reflect,
Which haunt my memories,
For in my heart, I will forever
        cherish my love.

EVESLACE

The pages turn,
Forever a warning,
Empty of reproach.

Time, the only thing in my favor,
Guided me days on end,
Each longer, each more silent.
No one knew of my flight,
Winding through the mazes to an island,
Suspended in time,
My sanction of rainbow shadows,
Reflections of light refrain.

Mountains pierce the sky,
Looming above the lush emerald,
A paradise, a lost Eden,
The colors deep and intense,
Fill the air with suspense.

Eyes are watching and waiting,
An ever presence behind my mind's eye.
Changes, moods, and dreams fill my body,
Pulsing through my veins.
I feel something or someone inside me
Growing stronger each day.

The air fell still.
A cold, eerie silence crept through this strange paradise
The skies turned gray as night sank into silent calm.

The clouds began to brew and boil,
The breeze sighed
As the earth retreated into the realm of its caverns,
Then welled up from the shadows,
Harkening to the depth of my soul,
It's voice piercing the darkness,
Calling from the storm.

Deafening echoes of silence beckoned me farther.
His call is the wind,
Calling, willing me to come,
Beckoning louder, louder!
The agony of resistance is unbearable,
To escape, my only thought.
I run for my life,
The wind tearing at my body,
The air so pure, it burns,
So cold and overpowering,
Chills to the very bone.
There's nowhere to go.
There's no escape.
I'm caught in a web,
Spun carefully and surely.

A sudden crash of thunder explodes.
A sense of timelessness floats through my body.
Faces whirl round and round,
Drifting into oblivion,
Whispering of gentle rains coming.

A voice in a whisper floats through the still,
Falling upon my ears, yet I don't know what he's saying.
I'm somewhere, a room.
A cool breeze stirs the air with scents of jasmine.
Sleep has dulled my body.

The room is silent now,
Light filtering through the windows.
Suddenly, I feel his presence,
The ever-watchful eye,
Eveslace is the name.
Welcome to paradise.

A sanctuary of sorts,
A creation untouched by man,
The earth within the cradle of time,
Born of Eden's grace,
Gifted of the mind of the chosen,
Gifted now of Eve,

Welcome to Eden,
Forever…graced.

A TIME OF COMING

What mortal says he cannot do this,
For each voice is He,
Each an echo within itself and its shadows.

Naught could it be for this great entity,
No life could there be greater than thine.

Rise up to thy beginning,
Seek only the birth of life itself,
Teach of thyself and understand,
Know the essence of thine own glory.

I know and am,
Yet none other can see.

They say only time will tell,
But what is to be said?
All the words have been spoken.
All have been written.
Nothing is left.

No one cares of life itself.
So little is left.
No love is spoken,
Only careful deceit,
Short-lived words of empty hearts.

O fury of fury, cast not the shadows of death
        upon thine Son
But breathe life to His weary bones,
For not He but mankind is the cause,
Each his own deceiver,
Lost in their iniquities.

Save thine Son of this earth of corruption.
Kindle the mighty wrath of justice.
Bring forth thine firm hand.
Let the armies of heaven unsheathe their swords
        of message upon the evil.
Rain forth the tears of sorrow upon
        this dark land.
Cleanse thine paradise of its plague.
Wash away the blood of the innocent
        from the land
That such as is evil of this land be lost in
        the maze of darkness
And new life be born of the Light.

RED SUN

An eagle, soaring free,
Cries to the moon winds,
Lifting wing on summer's flight,
Searching the deep shadows.

Stalking winds drift among mountain skies,
Whispering spirits of feathered rays,
Their silent tongues speaking the signs.

Soundless mirages of sun's design,
Fleeting glimpses, a lone wolf's cry,
Seek the answer to their call.

Lines of weathered time,
Fading skies of amber grace,
Mark their tales of legends great,
Through the ages weary of defeat.

Times past are only reflections,
Many moons drifting through the
        forbidden seasons,
The sweetness of a lifetime forever lost,
Massacred, stripped of a land once free.

Ever will there be the stains of bloodshed
        marring the earth,
The scars never to vanish
But to be forever remembered in the face of time,
A proud nation of dignity,
Forever banished.

DAYBREAK

To begin is to end,
For the end is begun.
Who is to say what will be.

The night brings the animals
Running rampant,
No limit to their destruction,
A great furor quakes the earth in a tremendous heave of agony.

Laughter, screams, nightmares of dream,
Void of face,
Void of soul
Cry out in havoc,
Cry out in agony of waiting.

Their paths, though different they be,
Run red against the sky of mourning.

Mist rises from the earth,
Hanging heavily in the gloom.
A forest, dark and gray, rises against the sky,
A foreboding forever.

A strange stillness filled the air,
A sound unlike any heard before,
The seas rose in gigantic pillars of foaming rage,
Slashing, gnarling all in its path.

With it the skies fell in dark anger,
A whirlwind of light shafted the core of darkness, ringing its plea.
It rose cold and monstrous from the eerie depths,
Shrouding the red skies in a towering column.

The earth groaned in a deep shudder,
Swelling and heaving.
The rising suns of morning's light
Shrank to the cold black of night.

Howling winds crept round, charred remnants of a world once filled
with life.
Haunting cries of horror fill the air,
Echoing in the silence.

No longer shines the sun,
Weary of ordeal,
But a shroud of dark lingering
On a quest unknown,
An aimless wanderer,
Again to begin another place, another time.

AGE

I've been too long sitting here, listening to myself.
All of the thoughts come back to haunt me.
I feel I can never escape the torment,
The pain I've felt for so many years.
I can't remember when I've been happy.
I can't even remember yesterday.

Time just passes me by.
I'm in a vacuum and can't get out.
No one hears my pleas.
No one sees me struggling.
Struggling, for what, so many say.

I know what to live for,
But no one sees.
I can't get anywhere.
I'm going around in circles.
I can't get out.

I have to free myself.
I can't let them do this to me.
I have to be heard in some way.
They have to release me.
For sanity's sake, they must let me go.

No one knows what I've gone through.
No one calls.
I'm only old,
And no one cares.

All of the years I fought to bring life,
All of the tears I shed for my loved ones,
Doesn't a lifetime of loving and caring matter,
Of working my fingers to the bone to put meals on the table,
To clothe and keep warm my children?
All of the smiles and laughter,
Were they false?

It seems so cold now,
So very distant,
As if I never was.

All of my hopes and dreams have vanished.
They're forever lost in light of day.
But in my heart, they'll always be,
For age is but time.
Yet to dream is a legacy forever to be cherished.
All I have left is this and no more.
Yet this is the most beautiful gift, never to be of mankind
But a legacy of heaven's divine light.

TRAINS AND COWBOYS

Too many years of going nowhere and being nothing
Have ended my life in anguish.

If I had only known how it was all going to turn,
I could have done something, anything, to change what I'd come to be.
I couldn't see them as I can now.

My younger days were warm and full of adventure,
Or I thought they were,
But I could never overcome my fears.

So many times, I tried to change,
Something always happened before I could,
Those long lonely nights of running,
I was so tired.
I couldn't face another day.
Then, the day came,
All the years of running, scratching together what life I could.
Every minute of pain and suffering vanished.
It was all like a dream,
A nightmare brought to light.

None of it mattered that day.
Nothing could.
It was all to end,
And welcome it was.

A man of truth came to comfort me,
But no words could rest my weary body,
Only the sound of silence filling the air,
Only after that last breath of life could I rest.

Then they came to take me.
In a long sigh of victory, I walked proud beside them.
I walked up those steps in dignity,
For I knew, though I had done wrong, I'd paid my dues,
And I'd been called to my reward.
I never killed a man, though they say many,
But only did what I was forced to do
By the very men who would condemn me.

I knew more in that last moment,
More than my whole life of running,
But it didn't matter.
I knew
I'd found my day.

GHOST TOWN

Eagles are soaring high above mountains in the sky.
The sun, a brilliant warrior, soars in a never-ending quest unknown.
Skies are there but fail to appear.
Bones bleached dry by the harsh reaches of emptiness array the sands,
Crying out to the nothingness,
Not a creature,
No life!
But only the cries, telling unheard stories to no one.

The wind blows relentlessly, unyielding to the sands,
Despairing, lost in a furious rage,
Wooden skeletons stand barren in the blazing heat.
Tumbleweeds fly through, as though trying to escape from a horrible unknown.
Hinges scream, boards moan,
There's a scream, a thud…and silence!

The air is thick with fear,
An eerie unknown stalks the streets.
Not a soul is to be seen.
The windows and doors are boarded to the intruder.
"Why doesn't he leave?"
"Who is he?"
"Why doesn't he leave us alone?"
"Go away!"
"Doesn't he hear us?"
"Leave, hurry, before it's too late…"

THE OLD MAN'S TALE

Music flowed soft and mellow through
the smoke-filled room.

Laughter drifted from some dark corner.
Glasses of amber flavored the air.

Many words were spoken.
Many tales told.

As the old man spoke, the aroma of the sea drifted through the room—
veiling it in a misty calm,
He told an eerie tale of the Dead Man's Sea,

Oh, the cold, shivering water, the Dead Man's Sea,
The skeletons of yore,
Beckoning, crying out.

The sea, cold and cruel,
Moans and whispers overall.

Tread carefully, Beware!
For the sea craves more.

The eerie depths hide death—who waits,
Dead, living, all, wait to seek revenge.

The mossy, corroding blackness, where
light dare not venture, hides the
skeletons of ships and crews.
In the darkness they walk…sighing,
moaning…

A wind from nowhere rages across
the darkness.
It carries their cries, whining through
the strange stillness.

As he finished his tale of strange, a
great shroud of darkness fell over the room.
A low, hideous laugh pierced the darkness,
An omen of warning!
The old man was gone!

SHADOWS ON THE WALL

People walking here and there,
Pushing, shoving, trying to get somewhere,

Lights of flashing wire,
The winds wind eerily through pillars of fire.
Ghostly shadows flow red against the night,
Fleeting glimpses of flight.

Shouts and screams fill the air
But fall nowhere.

Street cars, trains, and planes,
Right out their refrains.
People pushing, a massive crowd,
Grow loud, loud.

No one, nothing, nowhere,
No time to stop and stare,

Then there's no more,
For my mind is wanton to soar.

LEAVES

As he rose in the early morning light,
The sun shone bright.
Glowing warmly on her body as he looked down at her,
An inner strength rose inside of him, bringing memories of how they
were.
No other love had endured so many tears
Through so many years.

He bent over and kissed her lips.
She opened her eyes and smiled, touching his fingertips.
They looked at each other and embraced, never to part,
For the leaves of grass are many as the troubles of heart
But only to endure the strength of one's love to last,
Though many years have passed.

BLUE LACE

Lay me down beside the still waters.
Let not the waters be troubled.
Lay me down beneath the willow that weeps not.

Love me for me.
Love not a day without a heart, not an island of stone.

Let us be as the dandelion, following the music of the wind.
Let our souls be light, not burdened with the loads of time.

Lay my head upon the whispering dew of your body's caress.
As I lay my heart upon the sweetness of your soul,
Love me for tomorrow and tomorrow's sister.

When you are low, I shall lift you in my arms and love you better,
When there are no longer the tears of joy, but only those in the dark
        shadows of your eyes.
I shall bring light to those shadows.
I shall love you with my heart and soul,
As if there were nothing to quench the fire of love burning deep
        within me.
I shall love you but with my body,
With the gentleness none has felt before.

And as we rise in the pure light of the morn,
Let there be an everlasting impression of the moment,
Pressed deep within the pages of your memories.

All the Children

The most precious gift, the children,
Though they cannot walk to Him,
They are carried upon the wings of
    their loving devotion.
Their hearts, overflowing for joy of His
    smiles of sunshine and hope,
Turn the tears of sorrow to the wondrous
    gift of laughter.
They know that with each day, they grow
    closer to their dream come true,
To laugh and run, to play as others,
    to just walk!
Their hearts reach out with a love
    grand and glorious,
More pure and beautiful as time grows,
Grown before their time
Yet born of innocence.
The children are the blessed,
For they are His children.

THE GIFT

Though she had never told him, he knew that
    time was precious.
Each day was to be lived in love,
Each moment to be cherished forever.
A part of him was growing inside of her,
    and it was a beautiful gift,
A gift of her that would forever be a memory,
Each day more a part of her,
Her child, their child.

He spoke silently, through his eyes,
    deep with sorrow.
No word was needed, for the air carried
    the silence, the emptiness of his heart.
He lifted his face to heaven, and no more
    were there the tears but a sweet
    and gentle smile upon his lips.
All the many years of pain had vanished.
Only that moment, that rebirth of life
    mattered then.

ONLY REFLECTIONS

My heart cries out to you.
My body wavers for need of your love.
The sun remains, its warmth upon my soul,
    but nothing can fill the emptiness
     I feel within.

A fire burns, consuming all of my being.
Only ashes, stirred on the wind, call to my love,
Searching, should an ember fall and flicker
    to a flame,
If only to reflect within your eyes.
Or could it be only reflections,
Growing of my own need for the warmth
    of your body close to mine.

Each moment is an eternity of waiting.
When I'm in your arms all of time
    will stand still.

Yet I know it can never be.
Our lives are never to become one
    through all of time.
Only in my heart will our love be true.

FOREVER AND ALWAYS

Though the many times may be trying,
My love for you grows with each day.
Soon we shall be together as one.
Our lives only to begin.

Each moment we are apart,
My heart yearns for you.
My body feels the growing need for your love.
I worry many times of the day and night,
For my love is true.
I think of the many moments of laughter and love,
The times of need and understanding,

My soul, forever true to your love,
Will ever be a part of you and you a part of me.
Nothing could ever take this precious gift from me,
For without you, I could not live.
You are my love, my life,
Forever and always.

Never could my feelings change,
For my love is so deep and strong.
To share the rest of my life with you
Is my only desire,
For I love you with all my heart.

MAZES

I feel like I've been alive for all of time,
Though my youth is not far behind me.
I have lived many lives of war and rhyme,
Seen many times of past to be.

Time never ends my quest,
For I can never find my end
But have only my beginning at best
And the life of many wrongs to mend.

Each day is longer than the last,
Each dream more real.
Can I never end these nightmares of past?
Are there none to hear my appeal?

A multitude of voices cry out from my mind,
Longing to be free,
But their sanction they cannot find,
For it is never to be.

Their echoes, deafening to the ear,
Lend madness to the mind
And grow in overwhelming fear
Of reality, only to remind.

With each day, the more they grow,
So the present I cannot find,
Yet in my heart, the truth I know,
For each I am, but of one mind.

THE MIST

Skies slashed in awe
The cold blue stare,
Haunting mist, veiling the thaw,
Pierced by stark towers, looming from nowhere.

Each beckoning,
A giant reaching to heaven,
Embraced within the clouded ring,
The gift of the seven.

Given for a fragile moment,
Woven of angel's breath,
The bagpipe's haunting lament,
The mourn of Seth.

The echoing sounds grow intense,
Coming from nowhere yet everywhere,
Flowing endlessly within the silence,
Forming the essence of rare.

The bells chime their song of time,
Each the echo of another,
Growing from within their rhyme,
Words of heralding for their brother.

Winds whisper gentle thought,
Weaving a kaleidoscope of light.
Flickering flames of heaven wrought
Symbol of his might.

Shadows dance in allure,
Each a voice from among
All of time to endure,
Their heart's sorrow forever unsung.

From the mist rises the ring,
Wavering illusions of souls,
Offerings of the fragrant Tolu they bring,
For it is the source for whom the sexton tolls.

CHILDLESS MOON

The silent mourning of dawn's light veiling
    the forest in misty tears,
Sighs o'er the blackened emptiness of
    mankind's fears,

Her barren womb, a childless moon,
The ever-haunting soon,

Tears of sorrow wash down upon her
    flowing through rivers of fire,
Mourning her heart's desire.

Oceans of desolation scream in travail,
Shrouded in a misty veil.

The final jubilation,
Vanity's mirror of adoration,
Carry her on the winds of time,
Drifting endlessly in a quest of the sublime.

An eternity of waiting,
Unknowing what each day may bring,
If only her beginning to seek
The inheritance, the wrath her children wreak.

EULOGY

She lives on immortal,
Her life a gifted blessing,
An everlasting time immemorial,
A lingering remembrance shining forth
    through the darkness.

Those who mourn the loss
Are only sorrowful for their emptiness
    of heart
But are enriched by the presence of her
    undying life in memory.

Each moment past can never be lost,
Always to be found within the
    grasp of the mind.

Through time, the days fade in grace,
More distant with each coming year
Yet growing with love anew,
Forever reborn in each life begun.

THE NIGHT OF THE SUN

Each time I feel you near me.
My body quivers for want.

My life, no longer of loneliness,
Rejoices with love and happiness.

When moments of quiet enter my being,
My thoughts are always with you.

When loneliness may creep into my world,
Tears of fear flow through my eyes,
Tears for fear of losing my love
I've only began to find.

I begin to feel you near me within my heart,
And the tears disappear.
Again, my heart rejoices for your love,
Yearning to be forever yours.

A warmth rises within my body,
Drawing me closer to you.
Passion consumes me with a fire.

In the beginning, my feelings were unsure and lost.
I thought I could never say "I love you."
My mind was lost in a haze,
Until your love light pierced the shadows and
      found my heart,
Lifting me upon your sweet dreams,
The fire of your soul.

THE TREES OF TIME

In the book of old, it is written,
The message of time, through the sages,
Born not of man's device then.
They bear their gifts of blessing through
    the rock of the ages.

The earth shall open its depths to the darkness
    and swallow all that defiles the grace of their father,
And the light of dawn shall carry thine children
To the glory, the life of ever,
And in the new beginning, each shall be again.

Each reborn of flesh.
Their spirits born again
To begin another lifetime afresh,
Only to be brought to life again through
    the many times of men.

This gift I give, not of mankind but of myself,
    my soul, and heart.
This day I write of this blessed gift of life,
Of each to play their part,
But born into the bondage of strife.

The many children, true,
To bear the burden of each,
Their perfection they pursue,
Each born to carry and teach.

LOVE SHADOWS

Love is not a word nor a smile but an
    existence of thought and emotion.
This may be not apparent but an ominous
    cry in the night,
An unyielding stubbornness.
None can see such an existence.
By an unearthly tide of thought is there
    only one link
For beyond any creation of time.

My innermost thoughts cried to the
    hilt of the beckoning wind.,
My heart stayed to the raging torrents.
My soul soared high on the raven's cry.
Mine eyes are as the fawn of the dew.
Mine arms caress you as softly as down.
I hear you speak in whispers,
Touching me as the warmth of the rising sun.
My heart no longer stays but wavers
    to this newfound word.

THE GLADIATORS

Agony and sweat,
Burdens of the game,
For many there's no regret,
Yet for others there's no name.

The many faces of expectation
Crowded to watch and stare,
To see many a delegation
From here and there.

Brothers among men,
Once before this date,
Never to be again,
Their hearts filled with glare of hate.

To win the only thought,
To be in light of glory,
Never thinking of what's wrought,
Only to be the story.

Many just live to win.
Each day they prepare,
The words could never begin,
For none would care.

The pain of the defeated warrior,
For many, death is the same.
But for the winner, there's the roar,
The glory of the game.

WISTERIA

Raindrops are falling, cool and gentle.
As I look out the window,
I see memories of the past that I can never forget.

For many years, I've been living these memories
    over again and again.
I can't give them up.

There were days of wisteria and loneliness,
    never-ending in a lingering fragrance.
There were nights of quiet understanding.

My thoughts flow freely, unending—yet go nowhere.
I find bits and pieces.
Sometimes I remember only what we could have had.

Walking alone, thinking, feeling, seeing what has passed,
I know it can be again.

As the trees sway in the wind, and the rains come,
It will be as then.
Each day I come closer.
I can see you—

Your eyes with a haunting fire,
Your lips, moist with dew,
    kissed the sunshine with laughter
As a raven's cry was your hair.

I can feel that strange yet beautiful gentleness
     drawing me nearer.
You speak low and soft.
I no longer fear what is to come.

Walking with you, I am no longer.
I am but a memory of days beautiful
     and rapturous.
Memories of nights long forgotten,
But I can never forget…for I am
     no more, yet forever.

AUTUMN

When hues of summer become hues of autumn,
Leaves of green become goldenly awesome.
When skies of misty blue turn a graying hue
From the past of buried sorrow, love
    surges forth anew.

When days grow shorter, and nights grow longer,
New loves bond together as old loves
    grow still stronger.
Yet whether love is today, or love is tomorrow,
There will always be a bit of sorrow.

Though the many odds may grow,
Through each cloud, the winds blow,
Parting to bring the Light of the Son,
To guide and teach from the One.

With each season, the love strengthens.
As belief widens and deepens,
Time holds no boundary,
For love is infinity.

JULIE

The sun so bright and golden,
The moon so delicate and mellow,
My heart's vow is the wind's sweet melody.
My soul is the eerie beckoning of the sea.
I beckon unto you.
My sweet love, come to me.
My heart lies within my soul.
My soul is the wind and sea.

Forever my love shall we be one
For all of eternity,
For one is the blessed union of two,
Ordained by our beloved.
We are born of destiny,
Of each, of the other.

The Silence

Whether it cometh by sight or by sound,
It will be up to He,
There may be pain or none to be found
Or nothing to hear or see.

It may come soon or late,
But none can truly tell.
Only by the face of fate
May it be heaven or hell.

Death walks.
He waits, your every footstep in strife.
As all talks,
He counts away precious seconds of life.

He waits for those who dare tread
Upon the bounds of hell,
And Lucifer welcomes the evil dead,
Who have souls to sell.

As the candle of life
Slowly burns away,
Those living in strife
Have very little to say.

The end is near.
You wait the final light.
When the gates close on fear,
You gradually float from sight.

The sudden stillness
Followed by tear.
The small loving caress
Is filled with grief and fear.

CHRISTY

Sleep, sleep, my sweet child,
Sleep a gentle and loving sleep.
God will protect you from the woods of wild,
Though, in the many nights, sounds may creep.

Such a small bit of life I see,
So gentle, an angel sweet,
Never to know, I pray it be,
My Maker I must meet.

My life is but one.
They are two,
My husband and son,
My loves so true.

They must not be burdened with such sorrow.
They must be together always,
The bond of love to last through all the tomorrows,
Growing stronger with the passing days.

As time grows shorter,
I know I must leave.
I begin to remember the sweet laughter.
The feelings flow, softly rejoicing, never could they deceive.

Many moments there to last,
The more precious they grow,
Deep, within my heart, a treasure vast,
A simple gift yet forever a lasting
        memory of tomorrow.

A Friend, Mother

A helping hand,
Someone there in a time of need,

A shoulder to unburden upon,
Someone to understand and care,

Wearing the times hard and long,
Traveling the long road to love and
meeting its end,

A shining ray in the darkest of night,
Love in a very special way,
Someone with a talent rare,
A friend, mother.

CIRCLES OF LOVE

Though at times we both are angered and tired,
Our love will forever endure,
For in our hearts,
So true and lasting is our love for each other.

There are the sweet moments,
The quiet moments of togetherness,
And there are the tempestuous moments
        of laughter and love.

Each moment, whatever it may be,
I cherish with all my heart,
For no other could I love so much.
My love for you is deeper than the heavens,
Blessed by the divine Light.

The time we cannot be together
Seems like an eternity, never to end,
Yet in my heart, I know it's not true,
For I long for the moment I will be with you.
And I know it will be soon,
For nothing can keep us apart.

When I met you, I knew in my heart you
        were the one.
All my life, I have waited and been true.
I've waited for this moment,
The words in our hearts we vowed,
Never to part, not even in death,
Forever to be true.

Each day becomes more precious than the last.
Each day my love grows ever stronger,
Yearning for your body close to mine,
For your love to quench the fire within me,
To fulfill our divine purpose as one.

In my heart, I pray never to lose you,
For if it were,
I could not live.
I cannot live without your love.
For as we have vowed our love forever to endure,
We have become one.

When there is anger in your voice,
I feel the anger deep within me.
When there are tears of sorrow,
I feel this sadness.
The moments you are weary,
I feel this depression sinking deep within my heart
And yearn to help you.

Though I may try but not know how to help you,
In my heart, I pray for you each day,
Hoping, somehow, I can make you feel better.
There are truly no words that can
        describe my love.
Only heaven knows how deeply I
        feel for you.

For no other could I feel this way.
Forever I will love you with all
        my heart and soul,
Never to be untrue,
An eternity, our love as one.

THE RAPTURE

War storms rise to the occasion
To mark the beginning of an era,
Etched deeply within the record of life,
Come to pass as told long ago.

Dark nations rise,
Foreboding clouds, drifting,
Born again to wreak havoc across all they touch,
The touch of death's son,
The hand of blackness.

Eyes searching the sky for hope.
Children cry in their anguish.
No more tears are left to fall.
Only the siren song is heard,
The mournful wail of multitudes.

In this end, there shall be a beginning,
Though all the torment,
The wake of destruction,
Inevitable, as it is to be,
The Light shall come forth.

The heavens shall open,
And life will emerge
As from the womb of time,
And the Light shall touch the gifted,
Lifting them heavenward,
The gathering of the Rapture.

TROUBLED WORDS

My love is everlasting,
Each day, though it may be troubled,
I will love you always.

There are no other words I could say,
Only to repeat each over again,
Yet all is spoken in just one moment of love.

I feel weary of many things
The other night I wasn't leaving,
Yet I had to get away for a while.
Time alone was all I needed.

Your anger touched me deeply,
My heart aching,
Tears filling my soul.
I felt I was going out of my mind.
All I need is your love and understanding,

The tears overwhelming me,
I could no longer hold it back.
I felt so weary I couldn't control the emotions,
Each flowing within another,
Pouring out such sorrow.

Though your angry words cut my heart,
My love for you yearned for your
        tender touch.

The words of leaving broke my heart,
For if I would ever lose you,
My heart and soul would die.
I cannot live without you.

I need and love you more deeply than
words or emotion could ever express.

When you came and held me,
I felt ever closer to you.

My words, I can't control lately.
I just need your tender love and
helping hand.
I try with my all
To be good for you.
I could never be without you.
I need you and love you.

We vowed our lives to be one.
Forever, I pray, we shall.

MORE THAN YOU COULD EVER KNOW

We have little money and can do less,
But we have each other,
Our love and togetherness,
Our future to hope for.

All the money in the world,
It can't buy everything.
Only from the heart can love and giving,
    Friendship, and learning
        emerge as a gift of love.

Emotions that run deep within the heart,
The most precious,
Are more rare than all the gold and riches.

To express this gift each day,
To bathe in the Light of this warmth,
Is to grow and ever learn
To reach the highest of expectations and more.

Each kiss,
Each caress,
The loving touches
Are sweeter than the wines of old.

I love you more than you could ever know,
No less than our father.
Yet there are no words,
No boundaries to measure this most
    beautiful and rare essence.

If ever I would lose you,
My life would end,
For my heart would pine away,
Lost, ever searching for your love.

I will forever be yours,
For no other could fill the emptiness
	of my life.
No other could I love so much.
No other could I be a part of.
Forever my love will be true.
Never could it die.

BEYOND THE BARRIER

A time of no limit
Beyond the twinkling of eternity.
Resting in the womb of space,
The soul reaches out,
Grasping upon the threads of life.
It grows and nourishes,
Gaining the knowledge and wisdom of the
        many generations to come,
Ever constant in the search,
Perfection—the ultimation.

Yet to seek may never be to find,
For each guides their own destiny,
Though predestined their lives may seem,

Many times, the mind strays,
Reaching beyond the fringe of reality,
Groping within the confines of darkness,
For some, strength,
Others, needs to be fulfilled.

Many souls never find what they seek,
Forever lost in the whirlpool of their need,
The bondage from within.

DEATH SONG

Sleep has overcome me.
The candles slowly flicker.
Clothing me in darkness,
I travel the tunnel of life,
My metamorphosis of time's creation
Emerging slowly as a newborn,
Awakening to another dimension.

A feeling of loss, of overwhelming infinity,
    grasps me,
My mind whirls, faint with the
    gratitude of my being.

Voices greet me,
Lifting my spirit upon their sweet melody,
Guiding me onward,
Seeking the beginning, the ultimation,
Ever in search of the origin, the fin.

Now only soft winds whisper through
    the remnants.
Cold and stark, they stand in the night,
Staring across the emptiness,
Seeking consolation, a touch of remembrance.

The gleam in the light of the moon
Shadows their attire.
Forgotten in time's advance,
Forlorn silhouettes among the night sounds,
The earthen breezes carry their
      memories onward.
Though time passes evermore,
Speaking softly in whispers,
Drifting through the cold darkness,
They carry me onward.
My home I seek.

My father greets me with His loving hand,
A new life born of His Love,
An eternal gift more precious than time—
    I cherish.

STAR CHILD

I am a child,
Born not of this world
But a gift of the stars.
I am born a mortal body,
My soul an eternal gift I give,
My love, my Father.

My life I give through the windows of my soul,
My heart yearning for my home,
Lost in a world strange to me
Against my heart's true devotion.
I belong not to this world of iniquities.
I cry out through the words of my being,
Desperate for my beginnings,
For I fear my end.

Oh, agony of mankind,
Destroy me not.
I am not of your days
But caught in a time,
A time I cannot escape,
Caught in a never-ending nightmare
        of dreams.

Oh, my home, my eyes will never see,
Nor shall I touch the land I love so well
To feel the peace,
The gift of our Father.

HIS GIFT

He hath given me the gift of eyes
To perceive what others cannot
    through their gaze.
He hath given me the gift of ears
To behold what many cannot see past their fears.
He hath given me the gift of heart
To hope when many fail and part.
He hath given me a most precious
    gift of life
To feel His love within me lift—
    gone forever is my strife,
For I am reborn in His love,
My precious gift from above.

THE PAINTING

I see through the eyes of another.
I seek not this destiny,
For I am many, though I am few,
Yet I am one.
I soar upon the wings of a mind,
Eternal in a quest I search.
I rest not in my travels,
Nor weary do I grow
But younger and full of life.
Though age wearies my pallor,
My heart grows more precious
      in my endeavors.
My very soul reaches out to call,
Beckoning mystique,
Enveloping imagination.
With each new gaze,
Laughter of delight,
Frowns of distaste,
Each cherished moment
Brings life eternal to my very soul.

SELFISH MOON

Oh, selfish moon,
Rest not your weary head,
For nought could you
But to dream your dreams evermore.

Not of humanity could you know,
Nor of hearts love of giving.

Time has passed your door,
For gathering storms rage within.
Driving away, also, vows past given,
A solemn march of hearts mourning.

Oh, say you believe,
Yet in your depths you cannot.
Oh, rage, your staff,
Patience under feet, you tread deeply,
Unseen the pit your path leads.

Windows past,
Blow through their solemn breeze,
Echoing times long ago undone,
Mirrored from within.

Labors yet unfathomed,
Foster their seeds hidden,
Diminished through the darkness,
Weakens thy countenance light.

Yearn not, for none is to be found.
Gaze deeply, oh soul.
Dream deeply, oh heart.
Seek nought beyond but gaze within,
For the truth of vision mirrors
        within each ripple of thought.

MIRROR, MIRROR

Once there was a viper.
He had great visions of grandeur.
He dreamt of great riches and
      self-importance.

Day after day, he.would not, could not deter,
Not even a smidgen from his thoughts
      he thought so pure.
So full of happiness was he at a glance.

But, alas, to him it did not occur,
So much that he had to endure
Was not as he thought, not a chance.

Oh, how he now dreamed of a way, but
      only was there a blur,
He could not find the cure,
So his dream he continued to enhance.

He tried the feelings to bestir,
Oh, how he feared failure, but still
      he dreamed
To fly with the eagles perchance.
He tried so hard he became dizzier and dizzier,
Till no longer could he find the allure.
Around his head the butterflies
      began to dance.

He thought and thought, and it became
    Clearer.
He need only look within his heart
    to seek the answers truer,
For within himself, he found a gift
    greater than all the riches he
    could balance.

He found his true self—much greater
Than all his dreams could conjure.
He found the truth reflected within
    himself through his own countenance.

A BIRTHDAY WISH

A birthday is a celebration of the
     gift of life,
May this gift always blossom in
     your heart.
God bless!

Time goes by,
Yet youth stands forever,
A cherished gift given of eternal
     love and kindness,
Reflected within the mirror of your soul,
Always ready to shine,
A truth none can dispute.
Youth is the love and belief within
     your very heart
That none can take away,
For youth is eternal.

STARDUST

Pendulum jewels of shimmering radiance,
Cloak my heart's yearning,
For a time, long past,
Another time of being
Yet has not come.
A rebirth of spirit,
Glowing against a pallet of
      midnight hue,
Sings its serenade of eternal lights,
Beacons radiant,
Herald the age of new.

Echoes of Silence

I walked through the barren waste.
My heart sank in hopeless despair
As I watched the red sky veiled
 with a morning mist,
Creeping slowly across the land,
Stagnant with the smell of death.
Dawn no worse than the dead of night,
Its cries of agony and mournful
 howling swept over me.
Only the children, only the children,
They are all that is left to care.
No more the songbird to sing,
There's none to answer his cry…

POET

Words have no true meanings—
They are merely an instrument of each
    individual's creative imaginations,
Each an individual yet collective
    interpretation of one's own values.
Words are merely an instrument
    of the collective mind.
They are a symbolic representation
    of the intelligence.
Poetry is but a gift of words,
Expressed within the heart of each
    that reads it.
An emotion endless in its meaning,
Each word expresses its own individual
    and unique definition to each
    who reads it.
There is no one true meaning but
    an infinite wisdom of imagination.
This is the true gift of a poet.

I SEE, BUT DO OTHERS?

I can't seem to find myself.
I can't put the pieces together.
I'm lost, and it feels like I'll
      never be found again.
I'm falling, falling into the depths
      of darkness, down, down
      into an endless world swirling,
      whirling, spiraling into a
      timeless void.
There are no faces, no people—there's
      nothing but nothingness itself.

I feel so differently from others.
No one seems to understand how or
      why I feel these things.
I feel alone, lost around crowds.
I'd rather be in a quiet, peaceful,
      Beautiful place, where no other
      people are,
I need peace

To be in a quiet, peaceful spot, away
      from the chaos, the confusion,
To be beside a brook, under an oak,
      walking to nowhere from nowhere,
      feel the wind blow in your face.

Real peace is to be one with the universe,
     one with yourself and God,
Everything around us, all the beauty.
     we never stop to see it, smell it,
     touch it, to be with it.

But I see it, hear it, smell it.
No one sees this; no one sees me,
     for they cannot see what is
     true and simple.
No one cares what is true anymore.
No one sees past their own little worlds.

Life is too precious and beautiful to
     just pass it by.
The simple, gentle emotions are
     the most beautiful.
People just don't take the time to notice.

Truly, love and peace can be our
     only survival.
In love and peace, we can then
     find serenity, simplicity.

ANDROMEDA

As I gazed upon the misty seas, veiling
the lands of dawn,
I saw a light radiating from the heavens,
Flowing gently, softly lifting me into its arms.
I felt a quiet peacefulness.

Lights are flashing.
The winds are whining eerily through
pillars of fire,
Ghostly shadows red against the foreboding darkness.

Shimmering vessels of light streak the skies.
I see and hear but cannot move, cannot feel.
I sense only peace.
I know no fear.
I am as one with this world of unearthly tides
of thought
As the nights of darkness meet the suns
of morning, the moons of fire mellow.

A glow of cooling embers flows through the dawn.
An ashen hue envelops the misty void.
I flow as the winds of time to a new dimension.

RAINBOWS

The sun's warmth radiates from the heavens.
I hear my thoughts come to life in song,
Weaving their melodies through gardens of essence,
For the essence of thought is the essence of being.

Castles of my mind,
What is real or unreal,
All are one illusion.

Misty rays, rainbows glowing golden,
Pulsating, breathing life,
Soar high on gossamer wings
Through my soul of time,
For age is time, but to dream is forever.

Slow, slow,
Drifting aimless across the reaches of space,
Endlessly in moonbeams and sunny daydreams.

THE STORM

The blue beauty of the sky is turning gray.
The sun is slowly going down.
There's no longer the cool breeze.
There is a silent calm.

The clouds, fluffy and soft,
Become hideous, threatening black.
There is a strengthening breeze,
The leaves now show life.

It is so wonderful to feel the wind.
It harkens to the depth of your soul.
The storm calls in the distance.
The light flashes blindingly.

A voice beckons in the eve.
It calls from the storm.
The birds are no longer alive.
Nothing is; there's no sound.

The voice beckons you farther.
His call is the wind.
It blows and rages on.
You must go; you must.

Your will to go is overpowering.
He beckons louder, louder.
You run, run for your life.
The wind gets stronger.

Destiny calls louder, louder.
The storm is soon to break.
The air is so pure it burns your nostrils.
It chills you to the very bone.

There is a magnetic struggle,
All the earth, heaven, hell!
All heaven is pit against Satan.
It seems all earth is at its end.

There is a sudden blinding flash before you.
Your eyes are blinded a moment.
When all clears, a miracle is done.
"My love, my dream, you're alive!"

Heaven and destiny have brought this!
Now the wind is blowing softly,
All is in a hushing calm,
A pure, sweet, caressing rain falls.

WILD CHILD

Her eyes lied,
Cold in their blue stare.
Her bosom sighed
As she laid her soul bare.

His heart, though beguiled,
Knew the coldness of her heart.
Her nature, so wild,
Could only tear him apart.

She came to him so young and free,
His heart full of dreams.
But beyond her beauty, he could not see,
For deep within his heart, love reigned supreme.

Her eyes of indigo blue,
Now, soulfully, they stare,
Turning a grayish hue,
For deep within grows a spark rare.

The illusion she had sought
Once clouded by ego's guise.
Through the light, his eyes brought.
Now true love she could realize.

TRUE LOVE

Love can be a beautiful thing,
Or it can be heartbreaking.
It can make you sing,
Or your heart be ever aching.

Our love has been parted by war.
It is such a useless thing.
For it is so, so far
And such a beautiful spring.

There can be so much sorrow.
It seems just like a lore.
And there may be no tomorrow,
For I count the days o'er and o'er.

When the war had ended,
My love came to me.
And though many are dead,
I lived for the love of thee.

ONE MOMENT

One moment alone is a moment of silence,
No person to interfere,
Your station, a solitary fence,
And the sky the clearest of clear,

A cool breeze
Sways the tree bough.
A fragrance of lilac trees
Floats and weaves a blanket of down.

The fragrant air is the essence of spring.
It carries the sweetness of pure earth.
The air is so fresh and cool, you sing.
It brings to your soul a fresh and lively rebirth.

The flowers, the brightest of hues,
The grass, the mellowest of green,
All about is a sanctuary to you,
And it gives you a feeling serene.

An occasional passerby,
Cheerful and waves to greet you,
As he has passed, you breathe a sigh,
For your life is so sad and blue.

No one that passed could see
The loneliness deep within your heart.
No one is truly free,
Till his soul and body part.

Yet there may be peace to be found
In the purest of the day.
In the night of sound,
People say,

Live your own life.
Look to the Son.
Don't live in strife.
Be your heart and soul one.

An occasional saffron butterfly flits by,
Leaving a vivid impression
Of some long ago gone by
And a memory of a once warm sun.

The air becomes cold as the land.
It rustles the leaves so gently.
It's as though the gentle hands
Were caressing the ground and tree.

You walk your solitary walk.
The hues are golden as the sunlit dome.
Their silence is their talk
Of the past passerby since gone home.

They speak sweetly as the mother to her Son
And tell of a life I've never known.
So bright is the sun
That despite, it warms to the bone.

There never could be a day so sad
As when I walk alone,
But the talk of silence brings the glad
And brings home those who roam.

A dream is upon you,
And you awaken, again sad,
To see the dead of winter pursue,
Solitary, alone, and no longer glad.

A Bird, a Tree, the Sky, and a Song

Soar high, higher into the sky.
Be free and forever at peace.
No other paradise could you find.
No other sky with its arms opened so wide.
Fly away, little dove,
Find at home green and sweet as the
    morning dew.
Feel the gentle warm sunny breezes.
Soar high into the mountains.
Sense the pure air of the angel's breath,
The golden, endless warmth of love's devotion.
There you will find your peace.
You can sing as the golden lyre and harp
With so sweet a tune, too gentle for
    others to hear,
Only the dew itself and all it has kissed.
No other is there to hear but only you,
    the trees, and sky,
Heaven's greatest living mural, singing
    its sweet song of love to you.

CHILD OF THE WIND

Time passes, and our lives go on.
They take their own paths,
Though my destiny may not be as
    it should.
I will follow what my heart feels.
My melody is soft and rapturous.
It follows the motions of a breeze
    on a moonlight night, sweetly
    scented with dew.
I feel the gentle sway.
My mind and soul are drifting into
    the night sounds,
Flowing gradually into oblivion.
I am a tree.
I am the wind.
I am, and I am not.

WORDS

There are no words.
Nothing can show what is deep within
     your soul.
No one else is to see this book.
No one could possibly do so for it is not.

Whether there is dark or light, sorrow or
     happiness,
It is there, and more pages are filled.

From day to day, it becomes more
     intimately written,
A silent, lonely walk along the road,
The meeting in the park.
Spring is in the air, alive with sounds,
The long walks with him,
Laughing, crying, loving.

The pages are filled one by one
     until the last,
Then the book is no more.
It is but a passing memory.

ABOUT THE AUTHOR

Rita Thompson grew up in the small town of Boerne, Texas. She still lives in the home her father built. She has always had a love for nature and sees with her heart. Through her love for flowers, Rita became a florist and worked for fifty years, painting emotions with the flowers. Rita has since retired and enjoys her back porch with a cup of coffee. It is her sanctuary and peace to her soul; she enjoys its beauty with her several cats. Rita learned that her mother also wrote poetry with some of their titles being the same. She blessed her with the love and gift of writing. *Thank you, Mom*!

Printed in the USA
CPSIA information can be obtained
at www.ICGtesting.com
CBHW030813011124
16733CB00021B/317